Science Fiction and
Dreams

Corwin Howard Morton III MD, PHD.

authorHOUSE®

AuthorHouse™
1663 Liberty Drive
Bloomington, IN 47403
www.authorhouse.com
Phone: 1 (800) 839-8640

Published by AuthorHouse   03/31/2016

ISBN: 978-1-5246-0111-9 (sc)
ISBN: 978-1-5246-0110-2 (e)

For as long as man has been on this planet, he has looked upon the Stars and dreamt of a better tomorrow. And using his dreams with his imagination there came science fiction. and with science fiction came science fact Within These few stages, which we will talk about. It will be mentioned about some wonderful remarkable and frightening things that have taken place in the a few decades some that were thought to be impossible or just fantasy that have come true or nearly have come true. As well as many more possibilities that are on the way for the Future,

Although the science fiction genre is entertaining, it has raised many a question from time to time such as how can one make real working equipment out of this sci-fi fantasy?

Answer is: dreams and Imagination.

And if one figures out how to do that how will it benefit mankind?

Answer is: we don't know yet but when the time comes we will.

And in doing so how has science fiction inspired our youth from both yesteryear and today?

Well in answer to that: our youth have been inspired by joining NASA the National Air and Space Administration for one.

Learning all they can in many different medical fields, as well as doing all kinds of things in many different fields of Technology in the hopes to improve mankind in the process and make that better tomorrow today.

And as I said before Within These Pages we will discuss the most similarities & contradictions between reality science fiction and Imagination.

And it amazing how many things and ideas have come into real life applications, theories, as well as everyday items such as radio, television, and computers, cell phones, and of course the medical devices and the teaching tools and much much more...

And as a side note: it is equally amazing that if one wanted to take a book and read it and study it and live in it basically using their imagination and Escape into another world just by using no special powers just their imagination.

Science fiction, and Imagination as well as dreams, science fiction is the catalyst where is the imagination and Dream are what fuel our thoughts into creating things to keep us reaching For the stars so to speak in the attempts to improve mankind. and in doing so hopefully keep them tight enough to know more about ourselves in the long run.

Book Dedication

Corwin Howard Morton III MD, PhD a disabled veteran of sorts I'm somewhat of a multi-faceted man some have called me a renaissance man and I have taken time to dedicate this book you all the dreams, the engineers, as well as the Builders of tomorrow.

I also dedicate this book you my mother Judith Ann Flowers/ Morton / Hamilton like all mothers Stood By Me no matter what and thanks to her most of the time; even when I change the laws of physics and man. haha! I would surprise her by making things better temporarily if not permanent. also to Gene Roddenberry creator of Star Trek Wagon Train To the Stars was his idea. also to Irwin Allen creator of many other TV shows like 20000 Leagues Under the Sea etc.

As well as all the men and women who have died within the service of mankind and making these things happen and one of those people is astronaut Sally Ride who was the first female astronaut within the space program, and like me most of them kept their word.

More About The Author

Now this is my second book, as I said in my first book, I was raised in many different places and being that of an army brat I was brought up with many different animals as pets in my lifetime. and in my quest overcome what is known as The Impossible *as others have put it.* it quite possibly seem to please everyone including me that with my willpower I was able to push the limit's of my boundaries and abilities. and not only achieve what others said I could not but was able to create a new reality my reality, and in my reality can't is not a word and nothing is impossible only we can make things impossible for ourselves I not only studied my surroundings, as well as the many people and their mannerisms thereof, I also learned very much from my many pets over the years and in learning what I have with that of my acquaintances in the military as well as those I've inspired and have helped over the years I have learned the old saying *when life gives you lemons you make lemonade. in other words when the going gets tough, the tough get going never give up!* it can be confusing at times however, so be it and the harder it is to do it the more we have to try, however the important thing is never give up.

That's why when it comes to science fiction or anything really I put my all into it most of the time seeing that which

others do not see or do not wish to see that which is there, I slow down and take the time

Why?

Some say we live in a very busy and bustling world and they don't have time for a little stupid things in life they have to do what they have to do, however when the time comes for them to truly enjoy life it tends to be when it's too late.

Now in the pages that you read Beyond this you will find how science fiction and dreams, and Imaginations have brought many things into being as well as many advancements into things yet to be.

Now back in the early 19th century computers were big and bulky and took up half the room and they really didn't do that much and you had transistors and diodes not to mention vacuum tubes you had to constantly monitor and sometimes repair. Of course back in the early years of computers the governmental sector used them for defense and scientific purposes.

Then in the early 1960s young man by the name of Bill Gates built his own computer in his garage and out of that computer became a business known as Apple computers the computer is now a household necessity.

Web games, and a few short applications at first. A few years later when computers were understood a little bit more they became a learning tool in the schools help nurture and shape the minds of today's youth to help give them a little more to think about other than reading books and hoping they come up with more. solutions to the world's problems and in businesses to help in productivity also to help in efficiency as well as making a better product, and in hospitals to help in research and developments of new vaccines and medicines these are but a few of the computer applications that I speak of, and what were computers used for to begin with? well back in the 1500 computers were named abacuses and were widely used in China as counting devices.

And we have indeed come a long way from the big bulky computers of yesteryear to the home computers of today and the computers we use in schools and in businesses up to the computers that we use for travel in other things.

Where do you think these computers came from?

Well you can use your own conjecture in this! However I think computers came from science fiction and our imagination

why do I say that, because as I mentioned earlier the young man by the name of Bill Gates had a dream and invented something his garage. and like all things this something he invented was to be used for good and it probably was at first ultimately everything gets used for both good and bad,

Again why?

It has been said by Ricardo Montalban of Fantasy Island, it has been mentioned by William Shatner(Captain Kirk) Leonard Nimoy(Mr. Spock) and a whole slew of others throughout time that; because we do not take the time to understand and realize the life we have around us, <u>it is within Mankind's Destiny to destroy that which they do not understand which may ultimately lead to their own destruction however we can also change that</u>

That is a strong statement but it needs to be said; mankind has proven to have a strong will I know this because I have proven that now we take another step back intime understand the more upstanding tribes and people now the Incas, the Romans, and other races, like us were interested in the stars for guidance making maps for land and sea exploration and usually in these Maps were Land or sea monsters as well as many other details such as landscape. and in doing this they have come up with instruments that would help them. such as a string theory of sorts To help them with distance. and before they figured out that they used their hands and fingers for the correct measurements.

However even with these simple tools their navigation skills we're not always accurate, and so someone came up with a tool called a Sexton that is a navigational tool for maps and locations with this device one could take measurements from the air and from the sea as well as surrounding areas to determine

ones location. now the Sextant was somebody's dream that was made into a reality, which in turn helped a great many with navigational systems of the day. and although it was made a long time ago it is still being used today in some areas. and this is of course one such example all things that were once a dream in books and in science fiction however were made into reality.

Now let us move forward in time, we have all scene from the old movies with dinosaurs that roam the Earth so long ago. yet in late 20th century we are heard that through genetics that it may be possible for us to bring back the past meaning the dinosaurs in order that we might be able to study them a little better and a little farther back in time about the 50s we have the excitement of Flash Gordon and his science-fiction escapades this got us thinking about jetpacks and yes in about 10 or 15 years later someone created a jetpack and we began experimenting however it was deemed for use in the military only however in the movies jetpacks were used the everyday things and people in the sun movies, in others they were used for spy activity and covert Ops. another great thing that became a reality out of a dream that somebody had was that of a car a car that could double as a boat and I'm told in one case that doubled as a plane and that only works in the movies right now. because I'm told that was a reality it did work but not very well so it is back on the drawing board that one, and who knows sometime in the future it might come through again and actually work. as you see there are thinkers and dreamers Among Us always thinking of ways to make things better and like I said we have to remember that nothing is impossible as long as we put our minds to it we can accomplish anything although we

cannot discount the failures of today we must always look for tomorrow.

Now in the medical field scientists and doctors who watched science fiction shows, and read science fiction magazines we're equally challenged into making into reality sum of the vaccines, tools, and medical Therapies that are in use today and seeming as science fiction always changes the medicines, tools, and therapies always change there are a multitude of things when you think about it that we use today or are improving so that we can use tomorrow such as the bio bed systems in most of the science fiction movies and shows an early 60s maybe late fifties we began experimenting with cryogenics for use in spaceflight. we have scene computers grow From a Gadget in a garage to a big business tool and used in school systems and yes even in the home and quite possibly without science fiction and Imagination quite possibly none of this would have been possible and as I mentioned earlier because of Science Fiction magazines, books, and the imagination of our earlier medical profession we now have a multitude of vaccines and medications to treat the sick and afflicted, one of the only problems is money as well as if the product/ medicine will actually do what it says however at the same time as the saying goes:" *we're damned if we do and we're damned if we don't"!. basically it's a catch-22 situation.*

Then we have the medications that should have worked or the treatment that should have worked that didn't. or we have the opposite of the situation.

As we already mentioned we have computers in school and for those that are willing to learn computers can expand their knowledge and their minds to some extent however imagination, and dreams, Shall always play an important role in shaping our futures.

Now let's talk about the cell phone use in other communication devices again as far back as I can remember there were no phones to speak of, instead there was a messenger service and when I say this I mean the long distances there was Pony Express otherwise it was short distance you would hand write the note and deliver it in person a few years later we invented the telegraph I believe that was invented by Alexander Graham Bell incidentally a very short time later he invented the light bulb all these were thought to be impossible things to do however they were one man's dream and he made them come true, despite what everybody was telling him. now about this time in cartoons we had everybody stringing up cans and talking with everybody all over the place our work in cartoons would be a problem because nobody could walk anywhere without tripping over somebody else's piece of string haha.

But for us little kids that was a favorite toy two cans with a piece of string. the Alexander Graham Bell set out to invent the first telephone that would be used in the home. and because it was such a great hit, it eventually made its way into businesses, and schools and one of those businesses was the Bell Telephone Company which was always looking for ways to improve its phones and service.

In the meantime in the movies we were seeing movie characters like Flash Gordon, Buck Rogers, and Dick Tracy amongst many others talking on the wrist or transceiver belts

of course those were all rubber binders light bulbs and probably the multi colored cardboard but in later years we found that we were experimenting with possibly making them into reality and around the time of Lost in Space and Star Trek we came up with flip phones however they were big and bulky and they were with military to begin with before they were available to the public and the truth they were not flip phones. in time they got smaller and smaller and did eventually become what we know as a flip phone and as time progresses on and on they get smaller and smaller and each time that gets smaller the storage base gets bigger of course when this happens we also have computer chips that make this all possible, and at the same time computers have grown smaller and smaller with again more of a capacity to keep data the only downside to this is in some cases it becomes easier to break there is even talk of some day having a medical computer chip implanted in your hand so that when you go to the doctor all they need to do is scan your hand for your medical records.

Now let's talk transportation a long time ago it used to be if you wanted to get somewhere you had to walk, then somebody invented the wheel we think it was that a stone it might have been out of wood either way I don't think any of us really cares you either walked or you got a horse and trained it so that you could ride from place to place and then about the 15 or 16 hundreds somebody came up with an idea to make a wood-burning engine and out of that eventually I came up with locomotive a train that could carry passengers and cargo long distances.

That was soon to change, because it was found out later that it was more efficient and made the engine speed up a little faster if they used coal instead of wood and in some cases water was the catalyst in out of that came the steam engine. with the Advent of the steam engine through the inventor Robert Fuller we we got paddle boats on the river which could also transport Goods services and people too great distances in later years and with the Advent automobile now with the automobile this meant another Advantage people didn't have to travel in bunches anymore if you had an automobile you can travel by yourself or you can take one or two people with you in this honor for the automobile goes to Henry Ford the inventor and yes as time progresses we still look to the heavens for ways make the automobile a little bit better. but for now we have to deal with just the cartoons the dreams and the sci-fi shows, however someday soon.

We have airships, airplanes, air balloons, of all types and sizes psalm for Warfare, some for pleasure, in some for passenger travel purposes.

For instance I've learned that as far back as the middle of the Civil War or so balloons we use to spy on the enemy and to possibly drop bombs from above. and later about the early nineteen-hundreds that would put it in about the early 20th century Oroville and Wilbur Wright are credited with the invention of the airplane which was first to be a passing fad however it caught on as a way to get around in the air it was first used for airmail, then for sideshows and then with World War one coming up the potential of the airplane really took off it was used to rule the skies and take the war to the enemy in the skies as well as on the land.

However, when the war was over airplanes became just another thing for the dreamers and inventors look at new and better ways to improve this newfound thing called the airplane. Not only was it used for a strategic importance in many ways and improved upon over time, it also proved to be a modern time conveyance for public use in transportation purposes and of course this also was improved upon through the years. and yes despite all the problems we had and all the incidences had over the centuries most have been reassured that this is one of the safest ways to travel and see the world. and you see these are some of the dreams that were made into reality the things that were once in our imaginations or you could put it in the science fiction.

And they were all made into reality over time and improved on over time some of these things were forgotten and discarded over time being declared obsolete making room for the newer model.

Now as to submarines they first became dreams from different authors like HG wells, and Jules Verne to name a couple,

and one of the most famous submarines of all was depicted in 20,000 Leagues Under the Sea the name of the famous ship was the *Nautilus* and she was captained by Captain Nemo a man that was said to be tired of War tired of the senseless killing of mankind furthermore he was tired of Mankind's stride a perpetuation of sorts to make a better killing machine instead of trying to help all of mankind to strive to be better this of course is a classic book, but it is also a classic movie. and because of the book again we had dreamers who threw their imagination figured out how to make a submarine and make it work.

I believe one of the earliest cases making a one-man submarine at lease was back about the 18th century during the Civil War the submarine was very small and was a one-man Vessel and it was used mainly to attach landmines to the underside of the enemy's vessels in port, although these were very crude vessels and were not totally submerged they were made of wood often resembling large barrel's with a small piece of pipe or something giving an air tube, with a small gear shaft working very much like a bicycle that you had the pedal while you steered and once you reach the enemy vessel you would carefully Put a small explosive charge on the side of your enemy vessel and then you got the heck out of there as fast as I could otherwise he'd be caught up in the explosion because that was another invention we didn't have back then the timer, or the remote detonator and as time progressed this invention called the submarine also grew in size and dimensions as well as being a one-man craft start with it became a craft that could hold a great many Peoples who again were trained for war and later on or peacetime Ventures. and the submarines of today are well equipped to handle anything there is a fully functional sickbay

that has grown over the centuries from a one-room cabin do a fully functional what looks like a hospital Ward. as well as the submarines of today have not only bombs, but have torpedoes, as well as guns. and who knows according to science fiction they should also have lasers, and of course scientific equipment of all kinds, and of course ready for anything.

And of course with submarines we had to have land bombs and missile's, as well as many other weapons of mass destruction and we say we'll never use them yes we do.

Now we move into what was dreams and Fantasies only in our imaginations and in Books by such authors as CS Lewis, Jules Verne, Isaac Asimov, these are just a few of the well-known book authors that have brought space flight into the minds of the young the dreamers The Visionaries and one such visionary was that a Gene Roddenberry who brought this to life in a show called Star Trek, and what made this so very special everybody got along all Races of the world worked together and all Races that were found in the Galaxy lived together in peace, oh there were a couple of races in the galaxy that were afraid of change and did not want to be one of the pack so to speak but during these episodes of Trek, Lost in Space, space 1999 and a whole slew of others the world was excited to hear from our current president of the United States who said *" before this decade ends we must go to the Moon, and why must we go to the Moon? because it is there! and we do not do these things because they are easy, but because they are hard, and we will not do this because we must, we do this because we can."*

And because of this president *John F. Kennedy* one of many dreams was fulfilled actually had a moon landing on July 20th 1969. And although some say it was fake, Buzz Aldrin the first

astronaut to put a footprint on the Moon, sad to knows that to be true. I know this because I met Buzz Aldrin in the space conference that was held in Pasadena California I believe it was about 1990. in this meeting we had great discussion about the the future of space exploration and why after the moon landing of 1969 the most part space exploration was halted. And how we should get it back in action and hopefully get the public involved we also looked at former President Reagan's Star Wars program and took a second reevaluation of the freedom Space Station.

In this conference Buzz Aldrin was there Neil Armstrong was there as well as representatives from the Air Force, the Navy, and the Pentagon and I'm told this was televised on a Sci-Fi forum. it was a discussion made up of these fine gentleman and the General Public to raise questions as to why the Space Program basically closed down since the moon landing and the how we can generate interest again and getting it back up and running sending as in science fiction it never stopped running.

And we were basing that argument on *Star Trek, Battlestar Galactica* two very fine programs way back in the seventies who defined that the space program never halted it continued to find out what is out there!. and again another quote from John F Kennedy or former president *"we as a people must do this thing, for the good of ourselves because it is there"*. So with that being said it is our best interest that all the nations of the world come together and be as one so that we may accomplish this.

And with the support of the people and whatever else I am very glad that sometime in the 1990s I heard and saw on on several news networks as well as in Time Magazine, Newsweek, and a couple of others, that on a mission to Mars it was found that there were possible River beds with fossils with maybe

perhaps life there once they also found the famous face of Mars with no particular explanation of how it was made. and I was equally happy to hear the space station freedom was being assembled and that all the nations of the world that could afford to do so, we're contributing to the building of this station to work in conjunction with each other.

Despite our world problems, there are some of us on the Earth that believe Anything is Possible and there are some of us that believe you can do anything you wish to do if you put your mind to it and you want to accomplish it you will!, and it is People Like Us who actually make things happen for the good of mankind at least we tried. and some of us have died in the process of making the good things happen, and some of us still live to see another day and dream of a better way to do these things.

However, there are those Among Us if they can they will get a hold of the thing with the you have done for the good of mankind and turn them against us, as weapons of war. and it's up to us to stop so that we can keep moving forward, for this better tomorrow that we all seek to find.

So now it is time that I speak the reader of this book. I have given you a look into the past a small hint of History, and hopefully have inspired you to help us all make a better future. and I do hope you have enjoyed reading this book as much as I enjoyed writing it for you. and if you enjoyed it perhaps you'll check out things like the Smithsonian Institute, and the Air and Space Museum in Washington D. C. as well as your local Museums and of course syfy.com/ history.

And remember to always look and reach for the stars knowing that Anything is Possible thus nothing is impossible perhaps improbable at the time however eventually you will obtain it, and remember never let anyone tell you different. because if you put your mind to it you can do anything. thus achieving greatness in your own way.

It is said that science-fiction is nothing more than fantasy and although science fiction is for everybody to enjoy, we hopefully find some dreamers out there who will think of a better way for tomorrow and make it come true. because without dreamers there is no Syfy and without any Syfy we quite possibly would not have a reality--

Corwin Howard Morton the Third MD Ph.D.

Here are some other To checkout

The future directory: *an international listing and description of organizations and individuals active in the future studies and long-range planning.* compiled by John McHale and others.
Guildford, Surrey, Eng.: IPC Science and Technology press; Boulder Colorado Westview press, 1977

1. World future Society. The Future: a guide informational sources 2nd edition Washington DC future Society, circuit 1979

    And here is a guide you might enjoy on science fiction Tymn, Marshall, and others. *a research guide To science fiction studies*: an annotated checklist a peliminary and secondary sources. New York: Garland, 1977.

Indexes- Science Fiction

1. Contento William. *index to science fiction anthologies and collections. Boston: G. K. Hall, 1978*
2. *Fletcher, Marilyn P. science fiction story index, 1950 - 1979 2nd edition Chicago:* American Library Association, 1981
3. *Index stories in thematic anthologies of Science Fiction.* edited by Marshall B. Tymn and others. Boston: G. K. Hall 1978.